my DOG

edited by
Thomas Niederste-Werbeck

dogs

my DOG

teNeues

Previous page: my Dearg

DOGS is one-of-a-kind, just like your dog. As a sophisticated and at the same time informative as well as emotional magazine for dog-lovers, **DOGS** occupies an absolutely unique position in the German magazine market: A magazine all about the wonderful relationship between dogs and people! Like no other animal, dogs have been assigned practically worldwide the attributes of faithfulness and loyalty. Dogs are the oldest witnesses of our culture. This is what dog bones in Neolithic graves tell us. They have accompanied mankind for millennia and today they not only assume the role of best friend, they are also the partner in society and sports, the family dog and likewise companion. Ownership of a dog has many advantages. Not only in the way of social contacts: it is also proven that dogs have a positive affect on the health of their owners. Dog owners have fewer health problems, are fitter, less stressed and are often happier than people without a dog. Dogs have accompanied me from childhood on and are my great passion. Dogs bring fun, joy and happiness into our lives. I couldn't imagine a life without a dog. And naturally everybody thinks about his faithful friend: My dog is the best.

The response to **DOGS** magazine's call to send in the most beautiful shot of your dog was phenomenal, the editorial office received a veritable flood of photographs. Thousands were sent in, and in this book, which teNeues created in concert with **DOGS**, you will find our selection of funniest incidents, grand gestures and emotional moments. In images which are indeed superb, *my* **DOG** shows dogs from their best side. Your dogs!

Thomas Niederste-Werbeck
Editor-in-Chief, DOGS

DOGS ist unique, genau wir Ihr Hund. Als anspruchsvolles und zugleich informatives wie emotionales Magazin für Hundefreunde besetzt **DOGS** im deutschen Zeitschriftenmarkt eine absolut einzigartige Position: ein Magazin über die wunderbare Beziehung zwischen Hunden und Menschen! Wie keinem anderen Tier werden dem Hund fast auf der ganzen Welt die Attribute Treue und Loyalität zugeordnet. Hunde sind die ältesten Zeugen unserer Kultur. Davon erzählen Hundeknochen in neolithischen Gräbern. Sie begleiten uns Menschen seit Jahrtausenden und übernehmen heute nicht nur die Rolle des besten Freundes, sondern sind auch Sozial- und Sportpartner, Familienhund und Kamerad. Der Besitz eines Hundes hat viele Vorteile. Nicht nur den sozialer Kontakte, es ist auch erwiesen, dass Hunde die Gesundheit ihrer Besitzer auf eine positive Weise beeinflussen. Hundehalter haben weniger Gesundheitsprobleme, sind fitter, weniger gestresst und oft glücklicher als Menschen ohne Hund. Hunde begleiten mich von Kindesbeinen an und sind meine große Leidenschaft. Hunde bringen Spaß, Freude und Glück in unser Leben. Ich kann mir ein Leben ohne Hund nicht vorstellen. Und natürlich denkt jeder über seinen treuen Freund: mein Hund ist der Beste.

Die Resonanz auf den Aufruf der Zeitschrift **DOGS**, Ihr schönstes Hundefoto an die Redaktion zu schicken, war gewaltig, es folgte eine wahre Bilderflut. Aus tausenden von Einsendungen finden Sie in diesem Buch, das teNeues gemeinsam mit **DOGS** realisiert hat, unsere Auswahl der komischsten Momente, großen Gesten und emotionalen Augenblicke. *my* **DOG** zeigt in großartigen Bildern Hunde von den schönsten Seiten. Ihre Hunde!

Thomas Niederste-Werbeck
Chefredakteur DOGS

DOGS est unique, précisément comme votre chien. DOGS, en tant qu'exigeante revue tant informative qu'émotionnelle destinée aux amis du chien, occupe sur le marché des journaux allemand une position absolument unique : une revue sur les merveilleuses relations entre chiens et hommes ! Les attributs fidélité et loyauté sont attribués au chien comme à presque aucun autre animal dans le monde entier. Les chiens sont les plus anciens témoins de notre culture comme le prouvent des os de chien retrouvés dans les tombes néolithiques. Ils nous accompagnent, nous les hommes depuis des millénaires, et se chargent aujourd'hui non seulement du rôle du meilleur ami, mais ils sont aussi ses partenaires sportifs et sociaux, chien de famille et camarade. La possession d'un chien a beaucoup d'avantages. Et pas seulement au niveau des contacts sociaux : il est aussi prouvé que les chiens influencent d'une manière positive la santé de leurs propriétaires. Les propriétaires de chien ont moins de problèmes de santé, sont souvent plus heureux, plus sportifs et moins stressés que les personnes sans chien. Les chiens m'ont accompagné dès ma plus tendre enfance et sont ma grande passion. Les chiens apportent distraction, joie et bonheur dans notre vie. Je ne peux pas me représenter une vie sans chien. Et chacun pense naturellement à son ami fidèle : mon chien est le meilleur.

L'écho de la revue DOGS à son appel d'envoyer votre plus belle photo de chien à la rédaction a eu un écho énorme, suivi d'une véritable marée d'image. Extrait de ces milliers d'envois, vous trouverez dans ce livre, réalisé en commun par teNeues et DOGS, notre sélection des moments les plus comiques, des gestes les plus grands et des les plus instants émotionnels. *my* DOG montre les chiens de leur côté le plus beau avec des images fantastiques. Vos chiens !

Thomas Niederste-Werbeck
Rédacteur en chef DOGS

DOGS es única, igual que su perro. **DOGS** como revista exigente y al mismo tiempo informativa y emotiva para amigos del perro, ocupa en el mercado alemán de revistas una posición absolutamente singular: una revista sobre la relación maravillosa entre perros y seres humanos! Como a ningún otro animal se le adjudican al perro en casi todo el mundo los atributos de fidelidad y lealtad. Los perros son los testigos más antiguos de nuestra cultura. Sobre ello nos dan cuenta los huesos de perros hallados en las tumbas neolíticas. Ellos acompañan a los seres humanos desde hace siglos y asumen hoy no sólo el rol del mejor amigo, sino son también compañeros sociales y deportivos, perros de familia y camaradas. La posesión de un perro tiene muchas ventajas. No sólo para el contacto social; está demostrado también que los perros influyen en modo positivo sobre la salud de su patrón. Poseedores de perros tienen menos problemas de salud, están en mejor estado físico, menos estresados y frecuentemente son más felices que las personas que no tienen perro. Los perros me acompañan desde mi infancia y son mi gran pasión. Los perros traen a nuestra vida diversión, alegría y felicidad. No me podría imaginar la vida sin un perro. Y naturalmente cada uno piensa sobre su fiel amigo: mi perro es el mejor.

La resonancia a la convocatoria de la revista **DOGS** a enviar la foto más linda de su perro a la redacción fue gigantesca, prosiguió un verdadero torrente de fotos. De miles de envíos, encontrará usted en este libro –que teNeues ha realizado conjuntamente con **DOGS**– nuestra selección de los momentos más cómicos, grandes gestos e instantes emotivos. *my* **DOG** muestra en imágenes grandiosas perros del lado más lindo. Sus perros!

Thomas Niederste-Werbeck
Jefe redactor DOGS

DOGS è unico, proprio come il vostro cane. Come rivista pretenziosa e nel contempo informativa, nonché rivista emozionale per gli amici del cane, **DOGS** occupa nel mercato tedesco delle riviste una posizione assolutamente unica: una rivista sul rapporto meraviglioso tra il cane e l'uomo! Al cane, come a nessun altro animale, vengono attribuiti quasi in tutto il mondo gli attributi di fedeltà e lealtà. I cani sono i testimoni più vecchi della nostra cultura. Lo raccontano le ossa di cane delle tombe neolitiche. Accompagnano noi uomini da secoli e oggi assumono non solo il ruolo di migliore amico, bensì anche quello di partner sociale, sportivo, cane domestico e compagno. Possedere un cane ha molti vantaggi. Non solo il contatto sociale, è stato anche dimostrato che i cani influenzano in modo positivo la salute del proprio proprietario. I proprietari di cani hanno meno problemi di salute, sono più in forma, meno stressati e spesso più felici delle persone senza cani. I cani mi accompagnano sin dall'infanzia e sono la mia più grande passione. I cani portano divertimento, gioia e felicità alla nostra vita. Non posso immaginarmi una vita senza cani. E naturalmente tutti pensano al loro fedele amico: il mio cane è il migliore.

La risonanza all'invito di **DOGS**, di inviare alla redazione le foto del vostro cane più belle, è stata imponente, è seguito un vero e proprio profluvio di foto. Dalle mille spedizioni in questo libro che teNeues ha realizzato insieme a **DOGS**, trovate quanto abbiamo scelto dei momenti più spassosi, i grandi gesti e i momenti emozionali. *my* **DOG** mostra in magnifiche foto cani dalle parti più belle. I vostri cani!

Thomas Niederste-Werbeck
Caporedattore DOGS

my Emma

my Alfi

my Spencer
Previous page: my Molly, Sherly, Lana, Cooper and Lizzy

my Hedie

my Lotta

my Ally

my Nubia
Previous page: my Dalia, Caiba and Dante

my Victor

my Rica

my Tinto

my Charly
Previous page: my Valentina

my Henry

my Spencer

my Benny and Marlo

my Fisco
Previous page: my Pauli

my Wilma

my Spencer

my Maddox

my Spike

my Elfi

my Curtis

my Paula

my Lu, Peggy and Mango

my Shanti

my Laszlo

my Tibet, Piq and Tammy

my Dalia

my Paula

my Paula

my Max and Fine

my Chicco

my Fred

my Anni

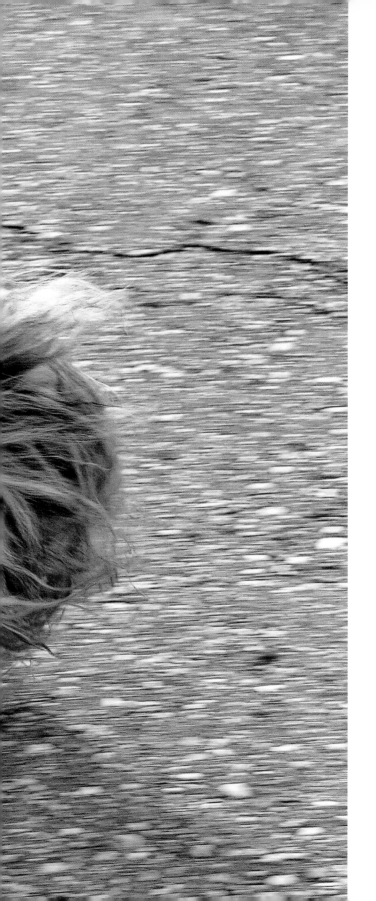

my Yuni

59

my Leni

my Carlo

my Donar

my Tubat

my Cleo

my Kate

my Jay-Jay

my Amy

my Silver Shayna's Djeeba

my Judy

my Mona

my Mickey

my Chinara

my Luna

my Khazir

my Emily

my Nero
Following page: my Candy

84

my DJ

my Enzo

my Amadeus

my Pauli

my Fine

my Grisu

my Lilli

my Camilla

my Cappy

my Zoe
Previous page: my Valentina

my Emilio

my Murphy

my Lumpi

my Ginger and Tiarè

my Randy

my Zoe

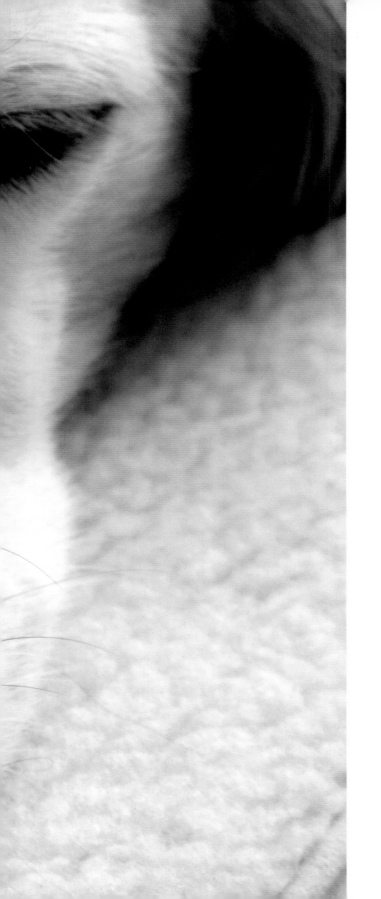

my Dana
Previous page left: my Theo
Previous page right: my Toto

115

my Arty

my Sina

my Flinn

my Enzo

my Fluse

my Oskar

Owner/Photographer

p 2: *Dearg* – Johannes Zimmermann

p 11: *Emma* – Anja and Klaus Mäder
(Owner), Thomas Post (Photographer)

pp 12–13: *Molly, Sherly, Lana, Cooper, Lizzy* –
Antonie Jamrowski

p 14: *Spencer* – Karsten Wilhelmus
p 15: *Alfi* – Annett and Steffen Ackermann

p 16: *Hedie* – Michael Punge
p 17: *Lotta* – Andrea Tuschke

pp 18–19: *Dalia, Caiba, Dante* –
Angelika Joswig

p 20: *Nubia* – Judy Hohmann
p 21: *Ally* – Christina Neander

p 22: *Rica* – Karin M. Erdtmann
p 23: *Victor* – Gudrun Krimbacher

p 24: *Valentina* – Katharina Voß-Ehlers
(Owner), Sabine Obst (Photographer)

p 26: *Charly* – Sarah Martens
p 27: *Tinto* – Justus Böckelmann

p 28: *Henry* – Anja Wick
p 29: *Spencer* – Karsten Wilhelmus

pp 30–31: *Pauli* – Jesko Wilke

p 32: *Fisco* – Lisa Kurz
p 33: *Benny and Marlo* – Alexander Bialas

p 34: *Wilma* – Moni Kranefoer
p 35: *Spencer* – Karsten Wilhelmus

pp 36–37: *Maddox* – Owner unknown

p 38: *Spike* – Liane Wolbrandt
p 39: *Elfi* – Owner unknown

p 41: *Curtis* – Andreas Arntz

pp 42–43: *Paula* – Kerstin Soer

p 44: *Lu, Peggy, Mango* – Anina Böttcher
p 45: *Shanti* – Katinka Bizer (Owner),
Thomas Post (Photographer)

p 46: *Laszlo* – N. Becker (Owner),
Brigitte Rühland (Photographer)
p 47: *Tibet, Piq, Tammy* – Ines Hohenbrink

pp 48–49: *Dalia* – Angelika Joswig

pp 50–51: *Paula* – Eva Schläfer and Jürgen
Bonigut (Owner), Rainer Spiller
(Photographer)

p 53: *Paula* – Temira Kronschnabl-Skiba

p 54: *Max and Fine* – Frank Henning
p 55: *Chicco* – Sabine Voigt

p 56: *Anni* – Margarete Singer
p 57: *Fred* – Rainer Spiller

pp 58–59: *Yuni (Ariyantas Yu-Ni)* –
Birgit Primig (Owner),
Georg Spitzer (Photographer)

p 61: *Leni* – Stephanie Grütz

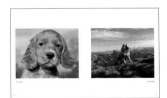

p 62: *Carlo* – Rainer Kohler (Owner),
Sabine Obst (Photographer)
p 63: *Donar* – Barbara Hubert

pp 64–65: *Tubat* – Eva Stammberger

p 66: *Cleo* – Sandra Truchly
p 67: *Kate* – Regine Niedermayr

p 68: *Amy* – Jessica Brodbeck
p 69: *Jay-Jay* – Sandra Lüdeke

pp 70–71: *Wilson* – Beate Konstantinou

p 72: *Silver Shayna's Djeeba* – Barbara and Thomas Post

p 74: *Alfi* – Annett and Steffen Ackermann
p 75: *Judy* – Marlene Geerts

p 76: *Mona* – Ursula Lueg-Althoff
p 77: *Mickey* – Gabriele Müller (Owner), Sabine Obst (Photographer)

pp 78–79: *Chinara vom Alesiatal* – Nicole Meckel

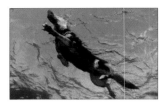

p 80: *Luna* – Andrea Schillings
p 81: *Khazir* – Constanze von Miquel

p 82: *Milly* – Christine Friederich
p 83: *Emily* – Karola Jacobs

pp 84–85: *Nero* – Bea Müller

pp 86–87: *Candy* – Constanze and Ulrich Zimmermann

p 88: *DJ* – Michael Esser
p 89: *Enzo* – Ursina Baitella

p 90: *Amadeus* – Fabian Katzer
p 91: *Pauli* – Jesko Wilke

pp 92–93: *Trüffel* – Ines Hohenbrink

p 94: *Grisu* – Anke Deeters
p 95: *Fine* – Frank Henning

p 96: *Lilli* – Andrea Kauth
p 97: *Camilla* – Katharina Niu

pp 98–99: *Valentina* – Katharina Voß-Ehlers (Owner), Sabine Obst (Photographer)

p 100: *Zoe* – Bine Bellmann
p 101: *Cappy* – Lisa Drescher

p 102: *Lilly* – Alexander Peppel
p 103: *Emilio* – Hanne Grothus

pp 104–105: *Murphy* – Mattias Steube

p 106: *Lumpi* – Silvia Bruderek
p 107: *Ginger and Tiarè* – Mareen Heymann
(Owner), Jette Huscher
(Photographer)

p 108: *Zoe* – Bine Bellmann
p 109: *Randy* – Ingo and Stefanie Könen

pp 110–111: *Kung Fu* – Julia Niessen
(Owner), Nicole Schultheis
(Photographer)

p 112: *Theo* – Sonja Gockel
p 113: *Toto* – Pascale Grote

pp 114–115: *Dana* – Petra Haltner

p 117: *Arty* – Martin Haasenritter

p 118: *Sina* – Bodo Gsedl
p 119: *Flinn* – Julia Christe

p 120: *Enzo* – Christian Karnatz
p 121: *Fluse* – Bine Bellmann

p 123: *Oskar* – Thomas Rode

Editorial: Thomas Niederste-Werbeck,
Lisa Nitzsche, Katharina Niu

Redaktion DOGS, Gruner + Jahr AG & Co KG,
Baumwall 11
20459 Hamburg, Germany
Phone: 0049-(0)40-3 70 30
e-mail: dogs@guj.de
www.dogs-magazin.de

Introduction by Thomas Niederste-Werbeck

Translations by ASCO International,
www.asco-international.de

Layout: Anika Leppkes, teNeues Verlag
Editorial coordination: Kristina Krüger, teNeues Verlag
Production: Alwine Krebber, teNeues Verlag
Color separation: Medien Team-Vreden, Germany

Cover: *Leni* – Stephanie Grütz

Back Cover: *Pauli* – Jesko Wilke

Bibliographic information published by Die Deutsche Bibliothek. Die Deutsche Bibliothek lists this publication in
the Deutsche Nationalbibliografie; detailed bibliographic
data is available in the Internet at http://dnb.ddb.de.

ISBN 978-3-8327-9216-9

Printed in Italy

Published by teNeues Publishing Group

teNeues Verlag GmbH + Co. KG
Am Selder 37, 47906 Kempen, Germany
Tel.: 0049-(0)2152-916-0, Fax: 0049-(0)2152-916-111
Press department: arehn@teneues.de

teNeues Publishing Company
16 West 22nd Street, New York, NY 10010, USA
Tel.: 001-212-627-9090, Fax: 001-212-627-9511

teNeues Publishing UK Ltd.
P.O. Box 402, West Byfleet, KT14 7ZF, Great Britain
Tel.: 0044-1932-403509, Fax: 0044-1932-403514

teNeues France S.A.R.L.
93, rue Bannier, 45000 Orléans, France
Tel.: 0033-2-38541071, Fax: 0033-2-38625340

www.teneues.com

teNeues Publishing Group
Kempen
Düsseldorf
London
Madrid
Milan
Munich
New York
Paris

teNeues